My
Organic Soul

Jacqueline Rhinehart

B *roadway Books* ■ *New York*

FROM PLATO TO CREFLO, EMERSON TO MLK, JESUS TO JAY-Z

My Organic Soul

A JOURNAL TO HELP

YOU DISCOVER YOURSELF

THROUGH WORDS OF WISDOM FROM VISIONARIES PAST & PRESENT

BROADWAY

Copyright © 2008 by Jacqueline Rhinehart

All Rights Reserved

Published in the United States by Broadway Books, an imprint of
The Doubelday Publishing Group, a division of Random House, Inc., New York.

www.broadwaybooks.com

Book design by Maria Carella

Library of Congress Cataloging-in-Publication Data
Rhinehart, Jacqueline.
My organic soul: from Plato to Creflo, Emerson to MLK, Jesus to Jay-Z: a journal to help you discover
yourself through words of wisdom from visionaries past and present/By Jacqueline Rhinehart.
p. cm.
1. Self-talk—Quotations, maxim, etc. 2. Hip-hop—Quotations, maxims, etc.
3. Success—Quotations, maxims, etc. 4. Conduct of life—Quotations, maxims, etc. I. Title.
BF697.5.S47R45 2008
158.1—dc22 2008013103

ISBN 978-0-7679-2976-9

PRINTED IN THE UNITED STATES OF AMERICA

1 3 5 7 9 10 8 6 4 2

FIRST EDITION

To my mother,

Maggie Lee Richards Rhinehart.

Thank you for encouraging me to talk to myself.

And to my father,

Willie James Rhinehart.

Because you are quick to listen and slow to speak.

Acknowledgments

THANK YOU

Janet Hill Talbert and Gwendolyn Quinn, whose efforts were indispensable.

Christian Nwachukwu Jr., for the title of my next book.

Lisa Brown, for the name of this one.

Verne Watley, I was listening.

The School of Practical Philosophy, NYC—my respite.

And to William and Felton—my talking brothers!

And to all those whose quotes are contained herein, thank you
for sharing your thoughts.

Foreword

Once upon a time New York City and its surrounding area was the epicenter for hip judgment. It was very common. Culturally quick thinkers and fast talkers, all cats mostly had were their heads and mouths. Brothers had so much game, dance, and rap before it was a term used for the music of hip-hop. Even women were accustomed to the skillful manner, the slick approach of the New York tongue and the New Yorker's wit. A lot of this was in the polite "air of things," and the words were requoted in the songs of artists and the pens of songwriters who gave bold commentary on the lives and the loves and the losses surrounding them. Our trust was to allow the artistry in our cribs to speak to us as if they were extended family members. It was safe enough or became a coda that played way over the mind of my little head. Yup, seemed like James Brown, Aretha Franklin, Curtis Mayfield, Ike and Tina Turner, Nina Simone, Odetta, Isaac Hayes, Stevie Wonder, and Gladys Knight were aunts and uncles singing in the house while I was doing house chores. The songs' titles and lyrics broke down further into catchy reminders of how we were not much different on either side of the record player. New Yorkers really were an underground network on what to take from those records and what the radio DJs were saying and then on reprogramming those words into life and lingo. They were quotes from and to "family."

It is no surprise to those of us who follow, comprehend, and retain that history that rap evolved from this same environment. It's a reason that rap started there. Not only were black and Latino New Yorkers talkers, but they were very knowledgeable about the cultural past too—griot-ish as that may sound. The ever eloquent Mr. Kool Moe Dee schooled emcees that they'd better "brush up" and build their vocabulary and intellect if they'd dare even think to battle him. Words were pure artillery in his opinion, used and matched with the quickness of high wit. The culture spread because something worked within its performance DNA. Of course, later businessmen smelled what was cooking in hip-hop's kitchen. Unfortunately the spread of intellect was dictated and tapered by the music's potential for financial gain. The result was that the most projected aspects of rap were similar to fast-food fries: great while hot, but processsed to fulfill for the moment. Not using the nutrients that the culture provided. Like throwing the fish away and trying to cook the bones.

Still, all and all, I'm such a believer in the recognition of the total contribution of the art form, because there's so much in those words. Words can help or hurt, or they can be neutral; words have inspired civilizations and sparked wars well before fighting the powers-that-be and contrived "beefs." My belief is the great majority of the rappers, writers, and emcees all say the most profound things, but when we wait for media and corporations to direct or mine the worth of what is said . . . we get a mutation of the craft.

When the words get brought out and explained, the rap world becomes every bit as fantastic as the NBA itself. Ms. Jackie Rhinehart's *My Organic Soul* shows the constructive beauty of the wit, charm, nerve, and power of today, yesterday, and tomorrow's millennial urban mindscape, albeit slowing down the verbal shrapnel that's often lost in much of today's speedy deliverance. That rap sensibility—in a hip-hop state of mind—happens to have spread throughout many facets of musical genre, life, and occupation. Yes, this has been fueled by the rap world in the past thirty years, but truly the sonic bites have always been lingering around as coda. My regret is that I really only know one language, although I have witnessed other skilled tongues do and say their thing on their local surrounding rhythms. Is it the beat or is it the words? We can continue to debate the cultural impact of rap, but when the words don't connect, there's absolute confusion on how to interpret what that vocal-less music really means.

Truth is, black artists have always been able to break it down. The preachers have always been quotable. What few politicians over the past 150 years we've had have always snatched a lyric or two from some of our greatest songwriters, singers, and poets. It sometimes appears like "gumbo in the air" because the phrases are cycled and recycled to give perspective to the art and create a foundation from which we can hear, and thus reuse when appropriate. The transhistorical truths of the lyrics examined here provide a great road map for life.

And so this book is both an accumulation and a recognition of inspiration from the past and for inspiration yet to come. *My Organic Soul* will possibly be a reintroduction of the words and logic of black artistry back into the black homes and even classrooms, be it if they dare. Bottom line: the "look out" love of the lyrics and music of artists— and especially black artists—within black music is chock-full of pointers, views, and quotes that seem basic but that save us in the end. I boldly state a lot of it starts right there and heads into other forms of music and culture threaded with the principles of honesty, straightforwardness, and a touch of historic reflection. But if we would only pay attention to the lyrics after the dance is over.

CHUCK D
PUBLIC ENEMY

My
Organic Soul

Introduction

It has always been my suspicion that people who say that they don't talk to themselves cannot be fully trusted—trusted to know the motivation, the "why" of their actions. Our knowledge is developed through listening: not only by listening to what others say, but by listening to what we say to ourselves. *So listen to your own thoughts.*

Yet with so much chatter in our heads, often we aren't even aware of what we've been told, until we speak out loud the words that have become embedded in our subconscious. Let this journal be your place to let those thoughts out. Like talking to yourself, this journal will hopefully lead you to a space where you unpack, hear, identify, and reflect upon the information—the ideological food—you've consumed. Each page contains a quote (or several) that will inspire you to reflect on the day you've experienced or snare you to ponder an idea, precept, or belief in your life. Reflect on these quotes and consider if they stand the test of experience. Each quote's power to inspire is intrinsic and self-contained—their arrangement is a reflection of this strength. That's why Jay-Z can stand beside James Baldwin; Salman Rushdie and Lauryn Hill are a breath away from the Book of Luke. Because labels often stop us from listening to and receiving truth, I have eschewed labels such as "negative" and "positive" and chosen quotes that were simply arresting and eye-opening. You may, therefore, find passages you consider sacred beside quotes you consider secular or provocative. There are no further directions included, but rather notations for you to gently consider and observe.

Be aware, as you write, not to censor yourself. Self-censoring is a roadblock to revelation. *Simply write.*

The purpose of life is to know oneself.

RICHARD WRIGHT

Even if
J-Hova witnesses,
he'll never testify.

JAY—Z

Consider: Getting to know yourself is an adventure. Although many people will witness your life, no one else can give your testimony.

Consider: A new year offers the chance to renew the self—to discover, to develop, to evolve. Once a friend announced, "The word for this year is 'process.'" The changing "self" is always a work in process, so consider that your only resolution is to be, as Prince once sang, "*willing to do the work.*"

The human self is not a gift; it is an achievement, not a static reality, but a painfully passed reality—past lions in the way, a triumph over ogres, real and imaginary.

JOSHUA LIEBMAN

I thought the ghetto was the worst that
    could happen to me
I'm glad I listened when my father was
    rapping to me
'cause back in the day they lived in caves,
    exiled from the original man
They strayed away
Now that's what I call hard times
I'd rather be here to exercise the mind.

RAKIM, "Ghetto"

*You can't run away from ya self, so that's
useless. If your word is bond, then you
don't have to make excuses.*

DEAD PREZ

I have to live with myself and so
I want to be fit for myself to know.
I want to be able as the days go by always to
Look myself straight in the eye!
I don't want to stand at the setting sun
And hate myself for the things I've done.
I want to go out with my head erect
I want to deserve everyone's respect.
But here in this struggle for fame and pelf*
I have to be able to like myself.
I don't want to look at myself and know
That I am bluster and bluff—an empty show.
I can never hide myself from me
I see what others may never see!
I know what others may never know!
I can never fool myself and so whatever happens
I want to be Self-respected and conscience free!

UNKNOWN

*pelf=money

Great men are they who see that spiritual is
stronger than any material force, that
thoughts rule the world.

RALPH WALDO EMERSON,
"Progress of Culture"

 **Consider:** There are many definitions for *word* in the dictionary: something said, talk, utterance, a verbal signal, a password, a saying, a proverb. Its usage is wide and varied—a word of God, Jesus was the "*word* made flesh," the Koran, the Bible, the Torah, the message, a news report, a promise. Look it up—it's all there. Whatever you decide is your definition, your words create and define your life. They have power. As a child, my grandmother would chide me not to repeat anything that I would not want to happen. "Don't give that *any life*," she'd say.

Consider changing your life by changing your speech.

Your words form your thinking—your thinking determines your emotions—your emotions affect your decisions—your decisions direct your actions—your actions form your habits—your habits become your character—your character = your destiny!

CREFLO DOLLAR

The beginning of wisdom is to call things by their proper names.

If names are not correct, language is not in accordance with the truth of things.

If language is not in accordance with the truth of things, affairs cannot be carried on to success.

Therefore a superior man considers it necessary that the names he uses may be spoken appropriate . . . that in his words there may be nothing incorrect.

CONFUCIUS

You are not Short, you are not Katt,
You're not a player or a pimp, Money stop that.
Learn to master your speech and be eloquent.

TALIB KWELI

"As-Salamu' Alaykum" is an Arabic-language greeting used in both Muslim and Christian cultures. It means "Peace be upon you." It is also transliterated as "Assalamu 'Alaikum" or "As-salaamu Alaikum." The traditional response is "wa'Alaykum As-Salam," meaning, "And on you be peace."

TRANSLATED BY ZARIFA MUHAMMAD

Create your own calm.

ERYKAH BADU

Observe: **How does your stillness affect others? Notice how you** *feel* **around agitated, nervous, aggressive people.**

God took a mess and made a message.

MARY J. BLIGE, award acceptance speech, New York

 **Consider:** There is no testimony without a test. What experiences have taken you to another level—will you share that insight?

Observe: The consequences of a test: (1) You know if you're ready. (2) You know your strengths and weaknesses. (3) You know if you're promoted. (4) Did you have the right tools and people with you? (5) You know the score.

And with all your getting—get understanding.

PROVERBS 4:7

Can't nothing make your life work
if you ain't the architect.

TERRY McMILLAN

Consider: Whatever it is you
are doing—is it *working* for you?

If you ain't speaking *your life*, your rhyme's adopted,
if it don't feel right then stop it.

BLACK THOUGHT OF THE ROOTS

The trouble with going with someone who has to find himself is that you've got to go everywhere they go.

DAVID G. EVANS

I *get around.*

TUPAC SHAKUR

And I'll be standing on the side *till you check it out*—when you get off your trip. Don't you worry 'bout a thing.

STEVIE WONDER

Observe: What am I searching for ? What am I grateful for?

Observe: When you feel an impulse to act, at what point does the action arise? Before taking action, remember—*you* are not what's going *on around you.* The real Man *is* the Spirit Man, and the Spirit Man is imperishable.

Don't push me, 'cause I'm close to the edge.
I'm trying not to lose my head.

GRANDMASTER FLASH & THE
FURIOUS FIVE, "The Message"

Man alone is double: mortal because of the body, immortal because of the real Man. For, although being immortal and having authority over all, he suffers mortal things which are subject to destiny.

THE WAY OF HERMES

There are three friends in life: courage, sense, and insight.

AFRICAN/HAUSA PROVERB

It is—what it is.

WENDY WILLIAMS

Consider: What is it that you have the courage to face, the sense to know, and the insight to understand?

Grandfather, Great Spirit,
Master of all things, you who are called by so many names,
and worshipped in so many ways;
allow me to become the Earth,
teach me to surrender to the tracks,
so that I may become that which I follow, and if I am worthy,
allow these tracks to lead me closer to you.

STALKING WOLF (Apache elder)

Consider: What "earth" do you want to become?
To what "track" are you devoted? And where will it lead you?

Consider: What do you understand that only firsthand experience could have taught you?

Ain't nothing like the real thing, baby.

ASHFORD & SIMPSON

A Wise man once said that trying to impart your understanding to others by talking is like trying to fill them up with bread by looking at them.

UNKNOWN

Our deepest fear is not that we are inadequate. Our deepest fear is that we are powerful beyond measure. It is **our light, not our darkness, that most frightens us.**

We ask ourselves, *who am I to be brilliant, gorgeous, talented, fabulous?* **Actually who are you not to be? You are a child of God;** *your playing small doesn't serve the world.*

There is nothing enlightened about shrinking *so that other people won't feel insecure around you.* We were born to make manifest the glory of God that is within us. It's not just in some of us; it's in everyone.

And as we let our light shine, we unconsciously give other people the permission to do the same. As we are liberated from our own fear, our presence automatically liberates others.

MARIANNE WILLIAMSON, *A Return to Love*

This little light of mine—
I'm gonna let it shine.

SPIRITUAL

SASHA.
The "stage" name Beyoncé calls herself
when she is in performance-character.

Everything I'm **not**
made me *everything I am.*

KANYE WEST

Free your mind . . .
and your ass will follow.

GEORGE CLINTON OF
PARLIAMENT FUNKADELIC

There is enough stuff
in me to make me a sinner
and saint.

DR. MARTIN
LUTHER KING, JR.

Consider: **Every choice to be one thing is a choice not to be something
else. We reduce our weaknesses by focusing on our strengths.**

As a man thinketh in his heart, so is he [or her].

PROVERBS 23:7

Consider: As you think, you act. What names and thoughts
have you told yourself today? What have you done as a result?

Consider: Life *may not* change. Consider changing *your mind.*

Nothing is as permanent as CHANGE.

UNKNOWN

Some things don't ever change.

TUPAC SHAKUR

You can't solve a problem
with the same mind that created it.

ALBERT EINSTEIN

I learn to relax in my room and escape from New York
And return through the womb of the world *as a thought.*

RAKIM

 **Consider:** Meditate by beginning or ending each day in stillness. Be still, sit comfortably and erect. Close your eyes and focus on the senses—feel the wood under your feet, the air on your face, your breath. Gently repeat your mantra [*om/ram* or your own single word]. Let the thoughts of your mind come and go with no attachment. Continue repeating your mantra and return when distracted *back to this word.* Begin the practice as a short pause between each activity during the day, and work up to longer periods of time.

Learn to be quiet enough to hear the sound
of the genuine within yourself so that you
can hear it in others.

MARIAN WRIGHT EDELMAN

If you cannot find peace within yourself,
you will never find it anywhere else.

MARVIN GAYE

Sometimes I sits and thinks and sometimes I just sits.

SATCHEL PAIGE (legendary baseball pitcher)

I'm just going to go sit with God and have a rest.

HUGH JACKMAN, actor, describing meditation on *Oprah*

People seek seclusion in the wilderness, by the seashore, or in the mountains—a dream you have cherished only too fondly yourself. But such fancies are wholly unworthy of a philosopher, since at any moment you choose you can retire within yourself. Nowhere can a person find a quieter or more untroubled retreat than in his own soul: above all, he possesses resources within himself, which he need only contemplate to secure immediate ease of mind. Avail yourself often then, of this retirement, and so continually renew yourself.

MARCUS AURELIUS, *Meditations*

The fool on the hill . . .
     THE BEATLES

Every man is a divinity in
disguise, a god playing the fool.
RALPH WALDO EMERSON

Train your mind to hear what you say.

CREFLO DOLLAR

My mind playing tricks on me.

GETO BOYS

Observe your thoughts. The mind can be a help or a distraction—watch your thoughts. Today, as Eckhart Tolle writes, "experience the shift in identity from being the *content of the mind* to being the *awareness in the background*."

Consider: Unforgiveness toward anyone (including yourself) is a blessing blocker—can't give none, won't get none. Consider dropping forgiveness like it's hot—the sooner we forgive, the quicker we stay in the flow of the receiving.

Get dropped like a bad habit.

DAMIAN MARLEY

Drop it like it's hot!

SNOOP DOGG

I tell you half the story, the rest you fill it in—
Long as the villain wins.

JAY-Z

Observe: In the script that is your life, what role are you playing? Are you typecast—or have you considered other possibilities? Could you go beyond the role of "villain," "good girl," "bad boy," "workaholic," etc.? Avoid labels and badges—they hinder possibilities, and they all wear out.

Consider: The Greek word for Power or Authority (*exousia*) contains the proposition *ex*, which means "out of" or "from." This suggests that the ability to influence change—to exert power—flows from *inside*. Power comes *out of* you. It is rooted in *what we are*. You have the power to change. "Do you wish to be great?" Augustine asked. "Then begin by being."

People do not wish to be worse, they really wish to *become better*, but they often *do not know how*.

JAMES BALDWIN

Power resides in the TRUTH *of who you are.*

SUZE ORMAN

Literature is the one place in any society where within the secrecy of our own heads, we can hear voices talking about everything in every possible way.

SALMAN RUSHDIE

It is written.

LUKE 4:4 (Jesus read too.)

Only through "the word" will enlightenment come. Be it the Bible, the Koran, the *Wall Street Journal, Spider-Man,* or *Essence,* you must read.

NELSON GEORGE, *Stop the Violence: Overcoming Self-Destruction*

Forgive us our trespasses as we forgive those that trespass against us—although, them again, we will never, never, never trust.

LAURYN HILL

Consider: Forgiveness does not necessarily mean restoration of a relationship.

Observe: How is the evidence of your childhood still present in your life?

It's a hard knock life for us.

JAY-Z

When you grow up the hard way
Sometimes you don't know
What's too good to be true
Just might be so.

LANGSTON HUGHES, "Madam and
Her Might-Have-Been"

Who explained *working hard may help you maintain,*
to learn to overcome the heartaches and pain.

WU-TANG CLAN, "C.R.E.A.M."

There is a period of life where we swallow a knowledge of ourselves and it becomes either good or sour inside.

                                       PEARL BAILEY

People who are oppressed are looking
for medicine—and cultural
expression is a medicine.

UNKNOWN

God gave me a voice to maintain my sanity.

GOSPEL CONTESTANT 106 on B.E.T. *Sunday Best*

Initiatory events are those that mark a man or a woman's life forever, that pull a person deeper into life than they would normally choose to go. Initiatory events are those that define who a person is, or cause some power to erupt from them, or strip everything from them until all that is left is their essential self.

MICHAEL MEADE, *Men and the Water of Life*

Consider: **Think about the significant events that mark your life. What happened to you? Who were your friends?**

We Bébé's Kids! We don't die, we multiply.

ROBIN HARRIS' BÉBÉ'S KIDS

We believe we are an *eternal* family.

DONNIE OSMOND

Have faith in you and the things you do
You won't go wrong, this is our family jewel.

SISTER SLEDGE

Observe: **What is your family's motto? What are the traits, beliefs, or legacy that you want to continue?**

Observe: How clearly do you see your dream? How present are you in this moment to life's possibilities?

Don't be afraid to close your eyes and dream,
And open your eyes and SEE.

SEAN "P. DIDDY" COMBS

To be *awake* is to be ALIVE.

I have never yet met a man who was *quite* AWAKE.

HENRY DAVID THOREAU

Between birth and death there is *the dash*—that's life.

DAMON DASH

Life is short and what we have to do must be done in the now.

AUDRE LORDE

This is one of the glories of man, the inventiveness of the human mind and the human spirit: Whenever life doesn't seem to give us a vision, we create one.

LORRAINE HANSBERRY

Consider: What does life really want from me? What are my gifts?

Shining star for you to see what your life Can Truly Be.

EARTH, WIND & FIRE

Observe: What are your dreams?

We were either going to start hip-hop
or *start a revolution.*

CURTIS "CAZ" BROWN

There's liable to be confusion in a dream deferred.
From river to river uptown and down, there's liable to
be confusion when a dream gets kicked around.

LANGSTON HUGHES, "Same in Blue"

> To accuse others for one's own misfortunes
> is a sign of want of education;
> To accuse oneself shows that one's education
> has begun;
> To accuse neither oneself nor others shows
> that one's education is complete.
>
> EPICTETUS (Greek philosopher, c. 50–120 A.D.)

Observe: **What have you learned that you must reevaluate?**

I think, therefore I am.

RENÉ DESCARTES, "Discourse
on Methods"

I am who I AM.

GOD'S REPLY TO MOSES ABOUT
HIS NAME, EXODUS 3:13

Consider: The words *I AM* signify continuous
Being, the immortal Spirit within you. I am is *life.*

The wisest men follow
their own direction.

EURIPIDES (Greek playwright)

I wish you insight so
you can see for yourself.

JAY-Z

Don't get involved unless you
feel a call, but when you do,
see it through.

MAHATMA GANDHI

Make it your ambition to lead a quiet life,
to mind your own business and to work
with your hands, just as we told you, so that
your daily life may win the respect of
outsiders and so that you will not be
dependent on anybody.

1 THESSALONIANS 5:14

Observe: Do your own duty as
prescribed, and do it perfectly—
and do not do the duty of another.

Jesus wept.

JOHN 11:35

To perceive is to suffer.

ARISTOTLE

Be kind, for everyone you meet
is fighting a hard battle.

SANDRA JOHNSON

*I've got to keep on pushing I can't stop now.
'Cause I've got my strength and it don't
make sense not to keep on pushing.*

CURTIS MAYFIELD AND THE IMPRESSIONS

The nature of man is not what he
is *born as*, but what he is *born for*.

ARISTOTLE

Consider: Hope is an
opportunity to push
beyond your apparent
circumstances.

*Tomorrow belongs to the
people who prepare for it today.*

MALCOLM X

*The best thing about the future
is that it only comes one day
at a time.*

ABRAHAM LINCOLN

Consider: What is the
one thing you can do
today to make your life
better tomorrow?

You don't have to get it, all you do is let it.

BROTHERS JOHNSON

Don't try—let. When you "try" to do things, you are working from the outside. When you "let" God do things through you, you are working from the inside and success must come.

ERIC BUTTERWORTH

A grateful mind is a great mind which
eventually attracts to itself great things.

PLATO

You can't hide from yourself—
everywhere you go—there you are!

TEDDY PENDERGRASS

Through the fire . . .
For the chance to be with you,
I'd gladly risk it all.

CHAKA KHAN,
"Through the Fire." Chaka says the "you"
she wrote of in this song was Jesus.

Consider: **What do you hope for? What
are you willing to go through the fire for?**

I think it's always worth it to stand on principle.

SUPREME COURT JUSTICE CLARENCE THOMAS

 **Consider:** To act on principle is to acknowledge that there is a value, an honor code, by which you abide, regardless of the circumstances or the varying opinions of others. To act in agreement with your knowledge of Truth is to act on the "strength of GP" (general principle).

Those who sow in tears
will reap in songs of joy.

PSALMS 126:5

Joy and pain,
It's like sunshine and rain.

FRANKIE BEVERLY & MAZE

Consider: Today, where necessary, cast off weakness and perform whatever action is right and necessary. Wisdom is avoiding all thoughts that weaken you.

Pain is just weakness leaving the body.

U.S. MARINE CORPS BILLBOARD, NEW YORK

Thank you, for lettin' me be myself—again.

SLY AND THE FAMILY STONE

People see you how you see yourself.

BISHOP T. D. JAKES

No person is your friend who demands your silence or denies your right to grow.

ALICE WALKER

Consider: Do you have the moral courage to accept yourself when others do not accept you for who you are?

I draw from every situation, everything I come across. That's something I feel really lucky in. I see everything and can apply it to everything else. I make a real easy correlation between things I don't think your average person can make correlations with. I'm always completely thrilled wherever I am.

MICHAEL STIPE OF R.E.M.

Observe: **Are you ever bored? Why? When?**

There is only one you
Can't nobody do it like you do.

FANTASIA

The freaks come out at night.

WHODINI

Consider: According to our fingerprints
and DNA, there is no one else on earth just
like you. How freaky is that? Do you dare
show the world how unique you are?

Consider: Everything you do in life requires a certain rhythm. Have you found yours?

With the *rhythm* it takes to dance
to what *we have to live through,*
You can dance underwater and not get wet.

PARLIAMENT, "Aqua Boogie"

It's the rhythm of life.

OLETA ADAMS

If you find your
rhythm, God will give
you the music.

T. D. JAKES

It takes twenty-one years to be twenty-one.

REGGIE JACKSON

We will serve no wine before its time.

ERNEST AND JULIO GALLO

Consider: You are a culmination of all your yesterdays. *Every day* you are changing—trust the process.

Greatness is not measured by what a man or woman accomplishes, but by the opposition he or she has overcome to reach his goals.

DOROTHY HEIGHT

I may have had some significance in my time because of the boundaries that I crossed that had ***not been crossed before.***

HARRY BELAFONTE

 **C**onsider: **Empathy is the ability to share and understand the feelings of another. Today consider the life of someone who came before you, as if that life were your own.**

When I was a child, I spoke like a child,
I thought like a child, I reasoned like a child.
When I became a man, I gave up childish ways,
For now we see as in a darkened mirror, but then face to face.
Now I know in part, then I shall understand fully,
Even as I have been fully *understood*.

1 CORINTHIANS 13:11–13

'Cause I'm just a soul whose intentions are good,
Oh Lord, please don't let me be misunderstood.

NINA SIMONE

It's not a matter of old school vs. new school. The point is I *went to school.*

SINBAD

Where there is no counsel, the people fall: but in the multitude of counselors there is safety.

PROVERBS 11:14

Only the educated are free.

EPICTETUS (Greek philosopher, c. 50–120 A.D.)

Consider: Life is an ongoing school. What are you learning today?

 **Consider**: You never arrive at a
particular destination by accident.
Where is your attitude taking you?

*Our attitude is the librarian of
our past, the speaker of our present,
and the prophet of our future.*

TAFFI DOLLAR

Don't put down the man with the better
hand, ol' Les trying to do the very best he can.

BOBBY WOMACK

It takes a nation of millions to hold us back.

PUBLIC ENEMY

I'm taking my freedom,
Putting it in my stroll . . .
Letting the joy unfold.

JILL SCOTT

I think myself happy.

ACTS 26:2

Consider: **Even joy requires discipline. You must decide to have joy.**

Express yourself!
You don't never need help from
nobody else.
All you got to do now is
Express yourself.

CHARLES WRIGHT & THE WATTS
103RD STREET RHYTHM BAND

When I liberate myself, I liberate
others. If you don't speak out ain't
nobody going to speak out for you.

FANNIE LOU HAMER

Consider: The world cannot accept
what it doesn't know. Tell the world
who you are. What are five fabulous
things you know about you?

Besides learning to see, there is another art to be learned—not to see what is not.

MARIA MITCHELL (American astronomer, 1818–89)

Don't believe the hype.

PUBLIC ENEMY

For the great majority of mankind are satisfied with
appearances, as though they were realities, and are often more
influenced by the things that *seem* than by those that *are*.

NICCOLÒ MACHIAVELLI (Italian statesman, 1469–1527)

I believe that the mind can be permanently profaned by
the habit of attending to trivial things. . . . Read not
the Times, read the Eternities.

HENRY DAVID THOREAU

 **Observe**: Think about the quality of information that influences your
reality. How often do you bury yourself (and others) in the grave of
public opinion? There is public opinion based on public trivia about
public personas.

You can hear other people's wisdom, but you've got to reevaluate the world for yourself.

MAE JEMISON

Does that make me *crazy*?

GNARLS BARKLEY

The greatest minds, as they are capable of the highest excellences, are open likewise to the greatest aberrations.

RENÉ DESCARTES

I am the product of the sustained indignation of a branded grandfather, the militant protest of my grandmother, the disciplined resentment of my father and mother, and the power of the mass action of the church.

ADAM CLAYTON POWELL, JR.

Be careful with hatred . . . Hatred is a passion requiring one hundred times the energy of love. Keep it for a cause, not an individual. Keep it for intolerance, injustice, stupidity. For hatred is the strength of the sensitive. Its power and its greatness depend on the selflessness of its use.

OLIVE MOORE (nineteenth-century English writer)

Don't hate the player—hate the game.

STREET PROVERB

Consider: Do you have an anger so righteous that it moves you to love?

Observe: What leaves you wide open? What exhilarates your soul?

We try to make our music so loose and hard-hitting
that it hits your soul hard enough to make it open.
It's like shock therapy.

JIMI HENDRIX

Most intellectual people do not believe in God, but they fear him just the same.

WILHELM REICH

Life commences not with birth, but with the onslaught of awareness.

W.E.B. DU BOIS

The two most important days of your life: the day you're born and the day you know why.

LIEUTENANT GENERAL RUSSEL L. HONORÉ,
U.S. Army (Retired)

Consider: Who are you?

When the soul uses the body as an instrument of perception, that is to say, when it uses the sense of sight or hearing or some other sense, she is dragged by the body into the region of the changeable and wanders and is confused; the world spins around her and she is like the drunkard, when she touches change.

But when she contemplates in herself, then she passes into another world, the region of purity and eternity, and immortality and unchangeableness, which are her kindred, and with them she ever lives, when she is by herself and is not hindered; then she ceases from her erring ways, and being in communion with the unchanging is unchanging.

And this state of the soul is called wisdom.

PLATO, *Phaedo*

You don't have to speak,
just seek . . . and peep the technique.

RAKIM

 **C**onsider: God does not obey us. He inspires us. Be still so that the activity of God can move you.

A man said to the world: "I exist."
And the world replied: "That fact has not created in me a sense of responsibility."

World, I will not change you all by myself, but I will contribute and you shall remember I passed this way.

REVEREND JIM HOLLEY

Life doesn't run away from nobody. Life runs at you and brings the best out of you . . . or the worst.

JOE FRAZIER

Consider: What is *life* bringing out in you?

Do not be too moral. You may cheat yourself out of much of life, so aim above morality. Be not simply good, be good for something . . . When you travel to the Celestial City, carry no letter of introduction. When you knock, ask to see God—none of his servants. In what concerns you much, do not think that you have companions, know that you are alone in the world.

HENRY DAVID THOREAU, letter, 1848

If you can't make a mistake,
you can't make anything.

MARVA COLLINS

 **C**onsider: Mistakes are exciting. Once they occur, you are closer to knowing what will work—because you know what doesn't. What would you do if you knew you could not fail? Do it.

What the caterpillar thinks is
the end of life, the butterfly
thinks is just the beginning.

UNKNOWN

Hide your purpose. The passions are the windows of the soul and practical wisdom call for acting . . . Even our wishes must not be voiced, so that they may not be met, by the one to deny them or by another to satisfy them.

BALTASAR GRACIÁN

Keep your dreams in a secret place.

REVEREND LESLIE SMITH WRIGHT

Observe: Today be mindful. Be aware of who you are and what you are doing *right now*. Sit still in a room for ten minutes, or take a walk and pay attention to your movements, the air, your breath, and what you see.

Most men pursue pleasure with such
breathless haste that they hurry past it.
                    SØREN KIERKEGAARD

Anticipate the good so that you may enjoy it.
                    ETHIOPIAN PROVERB

All eyes on me.

TUPAC SHAKUR

What was your original face—the one you
had before your parents gave birth to you?

ZEN KOAN

Authenticity is a kind of
courage; the authentic
individual faces something
which the unauthentic
individual is afraid to face.

JEAN-PAUL SARTRE

If you bring forth what is within you, what you bring forth will save you. If you do not bring forth what is within you, what you do not bring forth will destroy you.

JESUS, Gospel of Thomas

Do you.

RUSSELL SIMMONS

Consider: A great part of what happens in this life is dependent on what you do with what God has already given you—namely, *you.*

My name is Jimmy, and I want you to *Gimme*.

T. D. JAKES

They all stingy.
All these dudes know how to say is gimme.

JAY-Z

A man's gift makes room for him
and brings him before great men.

PROVERBS 18:16

Consider: Out of your belly flow the gifts of life. Since gifts come from
inside of you, nothing and no one outside will deliver you. If you
acknowledge and develop your own gift, it will take you exactly where
you are supposed to go in life. Success is awaiting your arrival.

Consider: Patience is exhibited when you continue to operate without deference to those irritations (attitudes, people, or situations) that deter you from your goal. Patience is the ability to persevere, while remaining in the same state of mind. Disregard others who pressure you to do anything other than *chill* and *patiently* run *your* race. Avoid comparing your life or mission with anyone else's. Instead, choose an heroic ideal to spur you on—to inspire you.

Who gives a *$@#!* about those . . .
Just *chill* 'till the next episode.

DR. DRE

Run with patience the race that is set before us [you].

HEBREWS 12:1

Haters, feel free to hate on me.

KATT WILLIAMS

Haters, get on your job—it's motivation.

T.I.

He who is not with me is against me.

MATTHEW 12:30

When you decide to do good—expect then all hell to break loose. The devil didn't care before—when you were on his side.

STEVE HARVEY

You gonna have to serve somebody, yes you are.
It may be the devil or it might be the Lord, but you gonna
have to serve somebody.

BOB DYLAN

When I submitted to God and made up my mind, it was like I was *between two opposing forces.*

IMMACULÉE ILIBAGIZA
(Rwanda genocide survivor and author, *Left to Tell)*

Choose for yourselves *this* day who you will serve.

JOSHUA 24:15

People are thinking I'm out here to avoid fame.
That's not it. What I'm trying to avoid is corruption.

DAVE CHAPPELLE, comedian, on his
$50 million "disappearance"

What shall it profit a man if he gain the whole world and lose his own soul?

MATTHEW 17:26

Check yourself—before you wreck yourself.

ICE CUBE

Every time you make a choice you are turning the central part of you, the part of you that chooses, *into something a little different from* what it was before.

C. S. LEWIS

If ain't nobody around you [to encourage you], you've got to learn how to talk to yourself. Act like you got somebody on the inside that knows something.

CREFLO DOLLAR

Do the Right Thing

    SPIKE LEE (film)

Try to do the more difficult right than the easier wrong.

GENERAL JAMES M. GAVIN (White officer who led
formerly all-black U.S. Army airborne troops to
become the first integrated 82nd Airborne)

Charming is what you are for the moment. Character is who you are all the time.

CREFLO DOLLAR

Consider: When you develop good character, you can relax and be yourself. For the next thirty days do the following; (1) Keep your word; (2) Do the harder right over the easier wrong; (3) Guard your principles; (4) Do the right thing.

Think—it ain't illegal yet.

GEORGE CLINTON
OF PARLIAMENT FUNKADELIC

I'm a public enemy, but I don't rob banks,
Don't use bullets, and don't use blanks.

CHUCK D OF PUBLIC ENEMY

We're not country. We're Southern.

OUTKAST

 **O**bserve: *How* do you listen? Listening without prejudice is a prerequisite to everyday listening. Without labeling or *prejudging* the speaker, listen only to the words, sensing the intention the speaker wishes to convey in the moment he is speaking. Then you are listening without prejudice.

Observe: Improvisation requires the musician to hear what's left unsaid, the notes not played, and space left between the beats of the music that's scripted. You improvise by playing what's unheard. Today listen and look for the spaces left open, the notes not played, the things not said.

Don't play what's there,
play what's not there.
MILES DAVIS

If love is a place I'm a go again, at least now, now I know to go within.

COMMON

Beauty is reflected in objects and in the observers who receive beauty through objects. If there were no beauty in the observer, then he would not find beauty outside. The mere fact that beauty is seen proves that there is beauty already present in the observer. Nowhere in creation does beauty stand by itself. The physical or sensory beauty has its foundation in the mental or subtle realm. The physical forms look beautiful because the mind is beautiful.

SRI SHANTANANDA SARASWATI

Try to see eye to eye 'cause love's not blind.
It knows when you care.

ANTHONY HAMILTON

When I'm alone in my room sometimes
I stare at the wall and in the back of my mind
I hear my conscience call. I need love.

                    LL COOL J

I travel the world and the seven seas
Everybody is looking for something.

          ANNIE LENNOX OF THE EURYTHMICS

The antidote to what is fundamentally wrong is the cultivation of what is fundamentally right.

MARIANNE WILLIAMSON

You can't get rid of bad habits.
You replace them with good ones.

DR. OZ

Everything is permissible, but not everything is beneficial.

1 CORINTHIANS 10:23

Discipline simply means moving freely.

SRI SHANTANANDA SARASWATI

Every habit and faculty is preserved and increased by its corresponding action.

EPICTETUS (Greek philosopher)

 **Consider:** Every habit, interest, talent, or proclivity you possess gets either better or worse depending on the time spent developing it. Separating the good from the bad influences in your life becomes easier when a discipline and a commitment to what is beneficial is established. Realizing all things are permissible but choosing more often to do what is beneficial can free life of many debilitating temptations.

For the love of money.

THE O'JAYS

*Thinking of a master plan—'cause
ain't nothing but sweat inside my hand.*

RAKIM

*To educate a person in mind but not
morals is to make a menace to society.*

THEODORE ROOSEVELT

You'd rather have a Lexus
or justice?

M 1 OF DEAD PREZ

Consider: For what price
would you change your
morals?

Quitting while you're ahead is not the same as quitting.

To conquer men is to have strength
To conquer oneself is to be stronger still,
And to know when you have enough is to be rich.

LAO-TZU (Chinese philosopher, founder of Taoism)

Observe: **What are your priorities?**

Ask him his dream, what does it mean?

"Can't be like *the rest*" is the most he'll confess.

CURTIS MAYFIELD

That's gangsta.
URBAN SLANG

We are the sons of Sorrow; we are the poets
And the prophets and the musicians.
We weave Raiment for the goddess from the threads of
Our hearts, and we fill the hands of the
Angels with the seeds of our inner selves.

You are the sons of the pursuit of earthly Gaiety.
You place your hearts in the hands of Emptiness,
for the hand's touch to Emptiness is smooth and inviting.

You reside in the house of Ignorance, for
In his house there is no mirror in which to
View your souls.

KAHLIL GIBRAN, "We and You"

Ready to Die

THE NOTORIOUS B.I.G. (album title)

Wearing the streets like they wear a crown
Wearing their dreams like they wear a frown
Riding in luxury with death on their minds
Is it coming tomorrow, should I open the blinds?

UMAR BIN HASSAN, "Bum Rush"

Consider: Your body cannot exist without a spirit. Yet death can be a state of mind if your spirit is numb. What is attempting to steal your joy, to kill your spirit?

I can play cool
But I can't play fool.

FABOLOUS

Avoid having your ego so close to
your position that when your position
falls, your ego goes with it.

COLIN POWELL

I don't like to preach too much. I like to get quiet, and then attack through my work.

DENZEL WASHINGTON

 **Observe:** How do you approach your work?

Respect the grind. Some n**@s want to be ballers *overnight.*

KATT WILLIAMS

No, I wasn't scared, because *you train first*, then you go for lessons, and *I was training for two years.*

JIMMY HAYWOOD, age eleven
(youngest African-American pilot to
make an international round-trip)

He who would learn to fly one day must first learn to stand and walk and run and climb and dance; one cannot fly into flying.

FRIEDRICH NIETZSCHE

Observe: In competition or conflict, how do you fight?

Women have balls in their heads where they are kept safe from blows below the belt.

NORMAN MAILER

You don't have to be an athlete to be a good sport.

MILDRED MORGAN BALL

You don't know until you're put under pressure. Across 110th Street is a hell of a tester.

BOBBY WOMACK

Observe: **What is putting pressure on you?**

It's okay to color outside the lines.

JIMI HENDRIX

You need to get you some good white friends.

KATT WILLIAMS

Getting to know someone, entering that new world, is an ultimate, irretrievable leap into the unknown.

ELDRIDGE CLEAVER

Consider: When you stretch and broaden your scope, your experiences and friendships will be broadened.

It's not your presents, it's your presence and essence.

ED O.G. & DA BULLDOGS,
"Be a Father to Your Child"

Consider: You leave the richest legacy in the things you can't see.

Consider: Give your full attention to the next person you encounter.

It's odd that you can get so anesthetized by your own pain or your own problem that you don't quite fully share the hell of someone close to you.

LADY BIRD JOHNSON

My anger wouldn't let me feel for a stranger.

TUPAC SHAKUR

*Love is an expression and assertion of self-esteem, a
response to one's own values in the person of another.*

AYN RAND

_____

_____

_____

_____

_____

_____

_____

_____

_____

Love thy neighbor as thyself.

MATTHEW 19:19

_____

_____

_____

_____

They do not truly love who do not show their love.

WILLIAM SHAKESPEARE

Because you're mine, I walk the line.

JOHNNY CASH

Teach me how to love . . .
How I can get my emotions involved.

MUSIQ SOULCHILD

It is a long long way
If you listen to your mind.
It is a short short way
If you listen to your heart.

MIRKO UDZENIJA

We are one.

FRANKIE BEVERLY AND MAZE

I celebrate myself, and sing myself,
And what I assume, you shall assume,
For every atom belongs to me
as good as belongs to you.

WALT WHITMAN, "Song of Myself"

One has to love "being *in a state of being*" to love
what is. To love oneself, before being able to love your
cat or God. To love is to be related to consciousness. It
is a realization that "You are I and *I am You.*"

WILLIAM SEGEL

Now I ain't saying she a gold digger,
But she ain't messing with no broke.

KANYE WEST

Don't want your mind, don't want your money,
These words I say, they may sound funny, but . . .

CHAKA KHAN

Consider: What does your love require?

Consider: Forgiveness does not mean the other person is right but that you are *free* from attachment to *whether they are right or not.*

They say all the right things to gain their position . . .
To shoot you down in the name of ambition they do.

LAURYN HILL

They smile in your face,
All the time they wanna take your place—the backstabbers.

THE O'JAYS

Everybody that's jealous of you is secretly scared of you. Their frustration becomes the inspiration for their hateration.

PASTOR LANCE WATSON

Even people you love will discourage
you and may not support your dream.

JONATHAN ADLER

Rock steady, rock steady, baby.

ARETHA FRANKLIN

My mother told me for thirteen years to go
get a good government job.

CATHY HUGHES (founder and owner of Radio
One and TV One, the first African-American
woman to head a publicly traded company)

An honest answer is like a
kiss on the lips.

PROVERBS 24:26

You can't handle the truth!

JACK NICHOLSON in *A Few Good Men*

 **Consider**: When you speak to others, are your words constructive and true, spoken kindly and in love? When speaking truth, be concerned with your audience. When giving constructive criticism, put your focus on what you love about the other person—not on what you don't. Observe when you say what you mean and when you don't.

Consider: Be cool, everywhere and in everything. Relax your effort, and any impositions of control, by accepting people as they are and allowing situations to take their own natural course.

Ain't understanding mellow.

JERRY BUTLER

Since I won't let critics seal my fate
They keep hollering I'm full of hate.
But they don't really hurt me none
'cause I'm doing good and having fun,
And fun to me is something bigger
than what those critics fail to figure.
Fun to me is lots of things.
And along with it some good I bring.
Yet while I'm busy helping my people
These critics keep writing I'm deceitful.
But I can take it on the chin
And that's the honest truth, my friend.
Now from Muhammad you just heard
The latest and truest word.
So when they ask you what's the latest,
Just say, "Ask Ali. He's still the greatest."

MUHAMMAD ALI

Say my name.

DESTINY'S CHILD

Who you calling a bitch?

QUEEN LATIFAH

If we are made in His image,
Then call us by our names.

ERYKAH BADU

In everything set them an example by doing what is good. In your teaching show integrity, seriousness, and soundness of speech that cannot be condemned, so that those who oppose you may be ashamed because they have nothing bad to say about us.

TITUS 2:7–8

Consider: **What is your name? What does it mean to you?**

Amid uproarious applause and admiration, Bill Russell was being honored by the Boston Celtics for his legendary achievements, including eleven NBA titles (as a player and coach) and an Olympic gold medal. On that occasion an historical video of his playing career was viewed. It included the racist taunts and jeers he suffered from his home crowd as one of the team's first black players. His daughter asked, "Daddy, how could you stand it?" And Bill said . . .

I didn't hear the boos, because
I didn't hear the cheers.

BILL RUSSELL, NBA legend

Consider: **Whose approval are you seeking? Will their disapproval stop your show?**

Look, I don't have the vision or the voice of Martin Luther King or James Baldwin or Jesse Jackson or even that of Jackie Robinson. I'm just an old ballplayer. But I learned a lot as a ballplayer. Among other things, I have learned that if you manage to make a name for yourself—and if you're black, believe me, it has to be a big name—then people will start listening to what you have to say. That was why it was so important to me to break the home record . . . I had to do it for Jackie and my people and myself and for everyone who ever called me a nigger.

HANK AARON, *Hank Aaron, A Biography*

Love you with a sense of purpose—*such a sense of purpose.*

THIRD WORLD

People are putting purpose to their purchase,
so we are putting purpose to our performance.

INDRA NOOYI (PepsiCo chairperson)

To have a purpose for which one will do almost anything except betray a friend—that is the final patent of nobility, the last formula of the Superman.

FRIEDRICH NIETZSCHE

Consider: **What is the real intention and motivation behind any action that takes place? Ask, why?**

Don't compromise yourself.
You are all you've got.

JANIS JOPLIN

Mama said knock you out
I'm gonna knock you out.

LL COOL J

 **C**onsider: Mothers are often our first "ultimate" authorities. Their instructions inspire us to do everything with a higher calling, a greater force. Today consider taking action as if for a higher calling. Do it for your mama or God.

If my train goes off the track . . .
pick it up, pick it up, pick it up!

BLACK SHEEP

You don't fight the darkness, you
switch on the light. If it goes out,
you switch it on again.

DEEPAK CHOPRA

Consider: Whatever action is required for you to do better, you will try, and try again.

It would not do for a student to answer every question of history by saying it was the finger of God. Not until we have gone as far as most in tidying up mundane events and the human drama are we permitted to bring in wider considerations.

EDWARD HALLETT CARR

When you pray—move your feet.

AFRICAN PROVERB

Faith, if it hath not works, is dead.

JAMES 2:17

Whether you're selling a dream, selling a scheme,
or playing a role
Like it or not we're selling soul.

CEE-LO

Got soul?

T-SHIRT QUOTE

*Feeling kinda' proud about the
product that I'm carrying.*

SLY AND ROBBIE

Consider: Does your "product"
(you) embody your values?

If we do all that is necessary, all the odds are in our favor.

HENRY KISSINGER

There is nothing like returning to a place that remains unchanged to find the ways in which you yourself have altered.

NELSON MANDELA, *A Long Walk to Freedom*

They caught the vapors.

BIZ MARKIE

Consider: Think about your authentic self. In a city unknown and alone, who would you choose to be?

For whatever a great man does, others imitate. People conform to the standard which he has set.

BHAGAVAD GITA

When I was hustling I had the same ambition they praise me for now. It was just the wrong direction.

50 CENT (CURTIS JACKSON)

*I have a great ability
to forget bad things.*

LEAH HORTON

The devil *does not want* your
stuff. He wants your joy!

JOYCE MEYERS

**O**bserve: **Your moods interplay always. But the spirit of you is the
unchanging Observer—your extension to the Creator. And while it sees
these emotions and moods, the Observer stands in view of them without
changing. Joy and wisdom come by avoiding all thoughts that weaken you.**

Live each moment like it's the last, and approach each task like it's the first.

QUINCY JONES

Nothing great was ever achieved without enthusiasm.

RALPH WALDO EMERSON

Both competition and cooperation are observed in nature. Natural selection is neither egotistic nor altruistic. It is, rather, opportunistic.

THEODOSIUS DOBZHANSKY

Get *in* where you *fit in.*

TOO SHORT

Observe: What are your gifts? Whatever they may be, identify what it is that you do well and with joy.

Notice the difference between what happens when a man says to himself, "I have failed three times" and what happens when he says, "I am a failure!" It is the difference between sanity and self-destruction.

S. I. HAYAKAWA

We all fall down—but we get up. A saint is just a sinner who fell down and got up!

DONNIE McCLURKIN

Now listen to the rule of the last inch. The realm of the last inch.

The job is almost finished, the goal almost attained, everything possible seems to have been achieved, every difficulty overcome—and yet the quality is just not there. The work needs more finish, perhaps further research. In that moment of weariness and self-satisfaction, the temptation is greatest to give up, not to strive for the peak of quality. That's the realm of the last inch.

Here the work is very, very complex, but it's also particularly valuable because it's done with the most perfect means.

The rule of the last inch is simply this—not to leave it undone. And not to put it off—because otherwise your mind loses touch with this realm. And not to mind how much time you spend on it, because the aim is not to finish the job quickly, but to reach perfection.

ALEXANDER SOLZHENITZYN, *The First Circle*

Mo' better.

SPIKE LEE

His pursuit of uncompromised detail made
me feel at times there was another me,
besides myself.

> TAKASHI MURAKAMI, famed Japanese artist,
> regarding his collaboration creating a
> Kanye West album cover

Ninety-nine and a half won't do.
TRADITIONAL BLACK GOSPEL SPIRITUAL

Between the failure and masterpiece is the distance of one millimeter.

PAUL GAUGUIN

If error is corrected whenever it is recognized as such, the path of error is the path of truth.

HANS REICHENBACH

Déjà vu, tell you what I'm gonna do, when they reminisce over you—my God.

C. L. SMOOTH

The mass of men lead lives of quiet desperation.

HENRY DAVID THOREAU

Consider: Write your own obituary as an exercise to discover the life you really want to live. Life is not a dress rehearsal. Are you performing the most important role you'll ever be given, the one you will be remembered for? *How ya' living?*

You are responsible for your own happiness.

JOEL OSTEEN

I always start out with a song for the day. The question is, will I keep it?

ANONYMOUS

Consider: What adjustment must I make to retain my equilibrium all day? Attempt to control not your circumstances but rather your reactions to them. Say no to negative thoughts.

I go for mine—I got to shine.
Welcome to the good life.

KANYE WEST

*You can't get to the end without
walking through the middle.*

JOYCE MEYERS

*There are no shortcuts to
any place worth going.*

BEVERLY SILLS

Consider: Wherever you are going requires
you to go through something. Don't be
deterred—the good life is a process.

We wear the mask.

LANGSTON HUGHES

Not one drop of my self-respect is
dependent on your acceptance of me.

QUINCY JONES, award acceptance speech, Los Angeles,
July 29, 2007, recalling what he and Ray Charles would
remind each other when faced with racism

A liar is a thief of the truth.

STEWART BOSLEY

Lying is an elementary means of self-defense.

SUSAN SONTAG

Integrity is the cornerstone of character and honesty is the core of integrity.

A. R. BERNARD

 **Observe:** When do you lie? Is there someone or something that appears to be more important than the truth? What premise are you defending? What do you fear?

How you climb up the mountain is just as important as how you get down the mountain. And so it is with life, which for many of us becomes one big gigantic test followed by one gigantic lesson. In the end, it all comes down to one word: grace. It's how you accept winning and losing, good luck and bad luck, the darkness and the light.

CHRISTINA CARLINO, *The Rainbow Connection*

It is not the load that breaks you down; it's the way you carry it.

LENA HORNE

Pimp juice is anything that attracts the opposite sex. I'm talking 'bout money, fame, or straight intellect. It don't matter see, women got pimp juice too—come to think about it, dirty, they got more than we do.

NELLY

Don't get drunk on your own juice. You ain't all that—it's Him (God)!

THE REVEREND DR. ZACHERY TIMS

Mo money, mo problems.

THE NOTORIOUS B.I.G.

For I have learned in whatsoever
state I am, therewith to be content.
I know how to be abased [without]
and abound [prosperity].

PHILIPPIANS 4:11–12

Consider: You can be discontent with money
and without money. What is your true source of
contentment? What increases your peace?

Most of us measure our success by what others haven't done.

TINA TURNER

Brush that dirt off
your shoulder.

JAY-Z

*People with good sense restrain
their anger; they earn esteem
by overlooking wrongs.*

PROVERBS 19:11

Keep your friends close and your enemies closer.

THE GODFATHER, PART 2

Pay attention to your enemies. They are the
first to discover your mistakes.

ANTISTHENE (Greek philosopher, 444–365 B.C.)

 **Consider**: All relationships are learning experiences. Even people who
withstand your ideas give you insight into your thoughts. If you choose to
consider your enemies as your teachers, your interactions—even brief
ones—will nevertheless be useful.

Your friends sweat you 'cause you ain't got
a band, but they don't understand some
things is meant to stay between a woman
and man.

TALIB KWELI

I know you *got soul.*

BOBBY BYRD AND JAMES BROWN

The Spirit searches all things, even the deep
things of God. For **who** among men *knows
the thoughts of a man except the man's spirit
within him?*

1 CORINTHIANS 2:15

Everything is copasetic.

BOJANGLES

I will not let you (or me) make me dishonest, insincere, emotionally tied up or constricted, or artificially nice and social, if I can help it.

EUGENE T. GENDLIN (philosopher)

How far must you go to gain respect? Umm
Well, its kinda simple, just remain your own or you'll be crazy, sad and alone.

Q-TIP

I don't know the key to success,
but the key to failure is trying
to please everybody.

BILL COSBY

Every effect that one produces gives
one an enemy. To be popular one
must be a mediocrity.

OSCAR WILDE

Equal makes the best friend.

AESOP

Have no friend not equal to yourself.

CONFUCIUS (Chinese philosopher, 551–479 B.C.)

The mind is lowered, O son, through the association with inferiors. With equals it attains equality, and with superiors superiority.

HITOPADESA (collection of Hindu writings, c. 500)

I have become all things to all men.

1 CORINTHIANS 9:22

Beneath the skin, beyond the
differing features and into
the true heart of being,
fundamentally, we are more
alike, my friend, than we
are unalike.

MAYA ANGELOU

 Consider: What is it that truly connects me
to others? What do equality, morality, and
freedom mean to me—and to my peeps?

Black, maybe?

Every man takes the limits of his own field of vision for the limits of the world.

ARTHUR SCHOPENHAUER

Observe: The limitations of your life are your own. Do you impose them on others?

For this dark diction
they've got an addiction.

KANYE WEST

Dear Momma, Wherever you are, if ever you hear the word "nigger" again, remember they are advertising my book.

DICK GREGORY, *Nigger: An Autobiography* (1964)

 **Consider:** In 1964, when Dick Gregory wrote this dedication for his autobiography, he knew the destructive power of a popular word. It was a word that his mother disdained, and it represented a mentality he disdained, so he took power over the word and his life. He sought to make a difference and change the system that used the word to destroy him. He would transform the word, he reasoned, as he had been transformed: "When we're through, Momma, there won't be any niggers anymore."

You can get with this or
you can get with that.

BLACK SHEEP

Progress is the friction of diverse minds working together.

PIERRE TEILHARD DE CHARDIN (French philosopher)

Consider: Right or wrong, whose conversation
makes you think? Who should you thank for
intellectually stimulating you?

When you face a crisis, you know who your true friends are.

EARVIN "MAGIC" JOHNSON

I pick my friends like I pick my fruit
My granny told me that when I was only a youth . . .
I don't walk around trying to be who I'm not
I don't waste my time trying to get what you got
I work at pleasing me 'cause I can't please you
And that's why I do what I do
My soul flies free like a willow tree
Ooohweee, ooohweee, ooohweee!

ERYKAH BADU, "Apple Tree"

You grew up with them clowns, ha . . .
now you stuck with them clowns, ha?

JUVENILE

Blessed is the man who walks not in the
counsel of the ungodly, nor stands in the way
of sinners, nor sits in the seat of the scornful,
but his delight is in the law of the Lord.

PSALMS 1:1

Get Rich or Die Tryin'

50 CENT (movie title)

I could be a pretty good thug, but it wouldn't compare to a great me.

CEE-LO

Do not wear yourself out to get rich; have the wisdom to show restraint.

PROVERBS 23:4

Consider: What kind of life am I really *dying* to have?

Consider: Do not accept whatever the world tells you. The hard drive of your mind can also catch a virus (wrong thinking). Are there junk files you should be deleting?

De-program and re-program.

GEORGE CLINTON
OF PARLIAMENT FUNKADELIC

In every situation and argument, watch out for the attractive distraction.

LAW SCHOOL PROFESSOR

Stick with your entrée and forget about the sides.

FABOLOUS

Observe: What is the 20 percent distraction that hinders your full appreciation of the 80 percent that you have?

Eighty-twenty.

T. D. JAKES

Observe: How often do you judge contents based on labels or packaging? Often we dismiss and reject someone because of their "packaging," and other times we accept people because of their packaging. How often are you fooled? Remember, Hitler was a vegetarian.

I am not my hair I am not this skin, I am not your expectations.

INDIA.ARIE

Now question: is every brother with dreads for the cause?
Is every man with gold for the fall? Naw, so don't get caught in appearance.

ANDRÉ 3000 OF OUTKAST

Trying to make it real—
compared to what?

RAY CHARLES

Let's talk about time travelin', rhyme javelin,
something mind unravelin'.

DRE OF OUTKAST

 **Observe:** What is the nature of your conversations? Are they about people, events, or ideas? Consider raising your conversation to the next level and keeping it real—with everyone (yourself included).

All great ideas are dangerous.

OSCAR WILDE

*Words are of course the most
powerful drug used by mankind.*

RUDYARD KIPLING (British poet
and 1907 Nobel Prize winner)

Observe: **The power of words can affect you in many ways.
Observe how they soothe you, anger you, motivate you, delight you,
enrich you, enlighten you.**

The true meaning of a term is to be found by observing what a man does with it, not by what he says about it.

P. W. BRIDGEMAN

It is the deed that teaches, not the name we give it.

GEORGE BERNARD SHAW

Consider: If actions do speak louder than words, exactly what are you saying?

Certain way I approached things I could
have done it with more tact and more class.

KANYE WEST on his 2007 MTV outburst

*A point of view can be a dangerous
luxury when substituted for insight
and understanding.*

MARSHALL McLUHAN

I dumb down for my audience to double my dollars
They try to criticize me for it but they keep hollerin'.

JAY-Z

*Nothing in the world is more
dangerous than a sincere ignorance
and conscientious stupidity.*

DR. MARTIN LUTHER KING, JR. (1963)

Not just in deep, she was total knee deep.

GEORGE CLINTON OF PARLIAMENT FUNKADELIC

You can only build as high as you have built low.
If the foundation isn't deep, the floors can't go too high.

T. D. JAKES

 **Consider**: How low can you go? How deep is your foundation?
Consider getting knee deep in something. Read, fortify, save, invest, build.

 **Observe:** Focus on yourself and consider the labels, identifications, and judgments you make.

An amateur built the ark, but professionals built the Titanic. Don't judge.

ANONYMOUS

Be open . . . My experience is that everything that's been huge, that's made me a lot of money, that broke records, God let me know it's not up to me, it's up to being open. If you're not open, like a parachute, you'll crash.

JOSEPH "REV. RUN" SIMMONS

The student of truth keeps an open mind, an open heart, and an open Bible.

ANONYMOUS

In my mind it is already a success.

ALICIA KEYS, on *As I Am* album release

If you have a goal, set it in your mind
Say to yourself, this will be mine!

D-TRAIN

Every good life contributes to the greater good life.

INDRA NOOYI (PepsiCo chairperson)

Be an asset to the collective.

SOUL II SOUL

I'm for truth, no matter who tells it.
I'm for justice, no matter who it's for or against . . .
I'm for whoever and whatever benefits humanity as a whole.

MALCOLM X

Everybody wants to be Black
until the cops come.

D. L. HUGHLEY

I know of no rights of race
superior to the rights of man.

FREDERICK DOUGLASS

Observe: Justice must matter *for* all if it is
to matter *at all,* for as Malcolm X once
observed, "Chickens do come home to roost."

Consider: Think about when to take action. According to Gandhi, when a major blow threatens to create a wound great enough to tear up the group that is following nonviolence, there is an obvious need to release the energy—*potentially violent energy*—in a manner that *disperses* the fuse but not the movement. *This* is the time to march. Dedicated to the march for the Jena 6.

When I move—You move
Just like that.

LUDACRIS

Exodus, movement of the people.

BOB MARLEY

Every generation must discover its mission and having discovered its mission—either fulfill it or betray it.

FRANTZ FANON

Visions are bestowed generationally.

T. D. JAKES

Consider: Don't let what you "see" today interfere with your vision of tomorrow.

Andrew Young once remarked that he and his friend Martin Luther King, Jr. "did not dream that in our lifetime I would have become the mayor of Atlanta or U.S. United Nations Ambassador."

I'm a survivor.

DESTINY'S CHILD

We, the black women of today,
must accept the full weight of a
legacy wrought in blood by our
mothers in chains . . . heirs to a
tradition to supreme perseverance
and heroic resistance.

ANGELA DAVIS

All the water in the ocean cannot
sink a ship unless it gets inside.

SUZANNE DE PASSE

Observe: What water is seeping into
your ship? Self-doubt? Insecurity?
Criticism? Focus on that which maintains
your contentment and honors your legacy.

Slave to the rhythm.

GRACE JONES

All actions take place in time by the interweaving of the forces of nature, but the man lost in selfish delusion thinks that he himself is the actor. But the man who knows the relation between the forces of nature and actions sees how forces of nature work upon other forces of nature and becomes not their slave.

THE GITA

 **O**bserve: **How has the rhythm of commerce increased your consumption of everything? Your resources can either support your freedom or make you an indentured slave. Today distinguish all purchases as either needs or wants.**

*An educated consumer
is our best customer.*

SYMS DEPARTMENT STORE

*Education makes people
easy to lead, but difficult
to drive; easy to govern,
but impossible to enslave.*

LORD HENRY PETER BROUGHAM
(Scottish statesman and historian)

Either move or be moved.

COLIN POWELL

Observe: A body at rest will remain at rest unless propelled by an outside force.

Consider: Make a decision and move.

[You] can't be too flirty, mama . . .
I know how to undress me.

PRINCE

Honey, it's easy to talk a good
game. What we need are folks
who will do something.

CONGRESSWOMAN MAXINE WATERS

Observe: **Conversations can be seductive and enjoyable, but action** *is*
the goal. It's not what you know but what *you do***. Today consider, as**
Percy (Master P) Miller would say, being "'bout it, 'bout it."

The Revolution will not be televised.

GIL SCOTT-HERON

Yo, I heard the revolution won't be televised but in the
land of milk and honey there's a date you gotta sell it by.

TALIB KWELI

The revolution is happening
in your apartment.

BILL COSBY

Man call *"this"* the third world.
Maybe it's just his *first* time around.

PAUL SIMON

We [Anglo-Saxons] are the first race in the
world, and the more of the world we inherit,
the better it is for the human race.

CECIL RHODES (British colonial statesman)

The world is white no longer and will
never be white again.

JAMES BALDWIN

 **Observe**: Perspective can be influenced by position. Practice altering your point of view to gain another perspective.

If you're Black, America is like the uncle that paid your way through college—but molested you.

CHRIS ROCK

I am the poor white, fooled and pushed apart,
I am the Negro, bearing slavery's scar,
I am the Red man driven from the land,
I am the immigrant clutching the hope I seek—
And finding only the same old stupid plan
Of dog eat dog, or mighty crush the weak. . . .
O, yes,
I say it plain,
America never was America to me,
And yet I swear this oath—
America will be!

LANGSTON HUGHES, "Let America Be America Again" (1938)

We shall have our manhood. We shall have it or the earth will be leveled by our attempt to get it.

ELDRIDGE CLEAVER

If we want this country to live up to its ideals we must stand and say uncategorically that we are a force to be reckoned with.

CYNTHIA McKINNEY (4th district representative, Georgia) in *American Blackout*

Consider: Think about the importance of the attitude and conduct of a person in a position of responsibility on *those affected* by him or her.

*When power corrupts,
poetry cleanses.*

JOHN F. KENNEDY

*The struggle is
beautiful. I'm too strong
for you to slave me.*

TALIB KWELI

Observe: What is your "poetic"
response to the stress of life?

We are positively a unique people, a breathtaking people. Anything we do, we do big! Despite attempts to stereotype us, we are crazy, individual, and uncontrollable people.

LEONTYNE PRICE

You know a flower that grow in the ghetto know more about survival than one from fresh meadows.

TALIB KWELI

Paid the cost to be the boss.

JAMES BROWN

Ask for what you want, and be
prepared to pay for what you get.

MAYA ANGELOU

Consider: All advantages
in life have their price.

Consider: How diverse are your options?

Education and money are very similar—all they do is buy options.

HILL HARPER

Change is certain, progress is not.

HILLARY CLINTON

Change has always been led by
those whose spirits are bigger
than their circumstances.

JESSE JACKSON, SR.

Society never changed. *We* changed it.

THE REVEREND AL SHARPTON

 **Consider**: Letting go of small things. Solving a problem requires you to get above it. Stay in what Buddhists call "Big Mind," allowing your consciousness to become bigger than your problems.

Thirty-one million dollars later, I didn't own it
[the Apollo Theater] anymore . . . But losing
money is not the most important thing in life,
making money is not the most important thing
in life, doing good with your money is the most
important thing in life.

MR. PERCY SUTTON

Waste neither time nor money, but use both
for your own and your neighbor's good. There
is no gain so sure as that which results from
economizing what you have.

Written on the wall of the Gotham Savings Bank

Consider: What good do you
want to do with your money?

To be possessed of a vigorous mind is not enough;
the prime requisite is rightly to apply it.

I came not to send peace, but a sword.

MATTHEW 10:34

The question is not whether we will be
extremists, but what kind of extremists we
will be. The nation and the world are in dire
need of creative extremists.

MARTIN LUTHER KING, JR. (1963)

Don't worry, be happy.

BOBBY McFERRIN

Observe: Funny, when my Mom heard Bobby McFerrin's popular song, she called and jokingly said she'd slap somebody if they sang it again! Not out of anger but because she perceived that song's sentiment—that the true meaning of happiness was to sit and idle away time—was ridiculous. Happiness, she believed, was a part of the process and often the reward for an achievement, not of what we've done but for who we've become— who we are. And who we are requires self-conquest, self-mastery, self-discipline. It requires critical thinking.

Here on earth God's work must truly be our own.

JOHN F. KENNEDY

Service is the rent you pay for room on this earth.

SHIRLEY CHISHOLM

Consider: Think about what your help means to someone else.

There is always something to do. There are hungry people to feed, naked people to clothe, sick people to comfort and make well. And while I don't expect you to save the world, I do think it's not asking much for you to love those with whom you sleep, share the happiness of those whom you call friend, encourage those among you who are visionary and remove from your life those who offer you depression, despair and disrespect.

NIKKI GIOVANNI

We all got a space to fill
everybody can't be on top,
but life it ain't real funky—
unless it's got that pop.

PRINCE

 **Consider:** Making a difference in life does not require a title or high position—it requires opportunity. Seize the opportunity to make a mark, to have an impact on the life of someone right where you are. Decide to make your life pop. You can make a difference and *fill a place*—not just a space.

CREDITS

ABOUT THE AUTHOR

Jacqueline Rhinehart is the president and founder of Organic Soul Multicultural Marketing, Inc., a firm that integrates entertainment concepts into creative marketing and branding opportunities. She is a masterful omni-media strategist, creating, developing, and implementing memorable campaigns in the music, entertainment, and lifestyle industries. She lives in Orange, New Jersey.